Blessings
and
Curses

Biblical Truth Simply Explained

Baptism in the Holy Spirit
Jack Hayford

Biblical Meditation
Campbell McAlpine

Blessings and Curses
Derek Prince

Deliverance
Bishop Graham Dow

Forgiveness
John Arnott

The Holy Spirit
Dr. Bob Gordon

Prayer
Joyce Huggett

Rejection
Steve Hepden

Spiritual Protection
Lance Lambert

The Trinity
Jack Hayford

Trust
Tom Marshall

Worship
Jack Hayford

Blessings and Curses

Derek Prince

Chosen Books
A Division of Baker Book House Co
Grand Rapids, Michigan 49516

Published by Chosen Books
a division of Baker Book House Company
P.O. Box 6287, Grand Rapids, MI 49516-6287
www.bakerbooks.com

Some material previously published in *Blessing or Curse: You Can Choose!*
by Chosen Books (1990, 2000)

Printed in the United States of America

Library of Congress Cataloging-in-Publication Data
Prince, Derek.
    [Explaining blessings & curses]
    Blessings and curses / Derek Prince.
        p. cm. — (Biblical truth simply explained)
    Originally published: Explaining blessings & curses. Tonbridge, Kent,
England : Sovereign World, 1994.
    ISBN 978-0-8007-9349-4
    1. Blessing and cursing in the Bible. I. Title. II. Series.

    BS680.B5P75 2003
    248—dc21
                                                                2003053056

Notes for study leaders

The topic of this book, blessings and curses, affects everyone in various ways. Do not be surprised if strong feelings and reactions arise during the study, particularly when answering certain questions.

As a leader you will need to balance the needs of individuals with those of the whole group. It is best to model an accepting attitude toward emotional responses. At the same time it is wise not to get side-tracked into devoting too much time to any one person in the group.

Some group members may be quick to rush in with advice or counsel for someone who is particularly struggling. That may not be the most helpful response, however, and may, in fact, be a way of defending themselves against their own difficult memories and feelings!

Our hope is that release, healing and blessing will come as people think and pray through the issues on their own and in the group setting. In some cases people will also need to take practical steps in response to what is taught. Some may well benefit from more counseling and prayer outside of the group, through the wider church.

Encourage group members to read one chapter prior to each meeting and think about the issues in advance. It is usually good to review the content of the particular chapter at the meeting, however, to refresh everyone's memory and so that those who have not managed to "do their homework" will not feel too embarrassed.

Five study questions at the end of each chapter will stimulate thought and encourage each person to consider how any of these issues may affect him personally. Praying together, asking for God's help, will help you to take hold of the truths presented.

May God bless you as you study this material yourself and lead others in doing so.

Contents

1   The Invisible Barrier   8

2   What Scripture Says   12

3   Moses' List of Blessings and Curses   18

4   Seven Indications of a Curse   23

5   No Curse without a Cause   28

6   Blessings and Curses through Authority Figures   35

7   Legitimate Curses from Servants of God   39

8   Self-Imposed Curses   43

9   Curses from Servants of Satan   48

10   Soulish Prayers or Utterances   52

11   The Divine Exchange   54

12   How to Pass from Curse to Blessing   58

The Prayer of Release   62

1

The Invisible Barrier

I believe this booklet can be of tremendous help to many people. The message it contains can change lives, communities, churches and even nations.

There are many people who are fighting something that they do not fully understand. Often they have an uncanny sense of stumbling just before reaching a long-sought goal. Something keeps them from leading a life of victory and fruitfulness.

I believe that in many cases, the problem is a curse over their lives.

A curse could be likened to a long, evil arm stretched out from the past. It rests upon people with a dark, oppressive force that inhibits the full expression of their personalities. It is an invisible barrier to receiving the blessings of the Christian life.

I myself was first led into this truth some years ago. I was conducting a deliverance service in a Presbyterian church in America when I noticed two parents and their teenage daughter. As I glanced at them, it seemed to me that the Holy Spirit said, "There's a curse over that family." I had no other reason for thinking such a thing. So I said to the father, "Sir, I believe God has shown me that there is a curse over your family. Would you like me to revoke that curse and release you from it, in the name of Jesus?"

To my surprise he immediately said, "Yes." I said a short, simple prayer. Although I was not in contact with any of them, there was a visible, physical reaction in each of them when I broke the curse in the name of Jesus. Then I noticed that the teenage girl had her left leg in a cast from above the thigh to the bottom of the foot. So I asked the father, "Would you like me to pray for the healing of your daughter?" And he said, "Yes. But you need to know that she has broken the same leg three times in eighteen months, and the doctors say it will not heal."

Today if I heard that a person had broken the same leg three times in eighteen months, it would immediately set off warning bells in my mind, alerting me that a curse could be at work. At that time, however, I did not see any connection between a curse and such an unnatural series of accidents. I held the cast in my hands and prayed a simple prayer for healing.

Shortly afterwards, I got a letter thanking me for what had happened and saying that when they went back to the health clinic, the X ray showed that the leg had healed, and the daughter was soon out of the cast. The father also told me about a series of strange, unhappy incidents affecting the life of his family, which is why he was so ready to acknowledge the need for the whole family to be released from a curse.

As I meditated on that experience, I realized that God had led me to break the curse over the family before He permitted me to pray for the healing of the daughter. I believe that she could not have been healed until the curse was revoked. In other words, the curse was an invisible barrier that kept her from the blessing that God wanted her to receive.

As I turned to the Scriptures, I was amazed by how much the Bible has to say about blessings and curses, and how little I had heard preached about them.

An incident in my own life tied in with all this. In 1904 my maternal grandfather had commanded a British expeditionary force sent to suppress the Boxer Rebellion in China. He had returned with various pieces of Chinese art, some of which passed to me in 1970 after the death of my mother. Among them was a set of four exquisitely embroidered dragons, which found a place of honor in our living room. These purple and scarlet dragons had five claws on each foot, indicating that they were "imperial" dragons. Because my grandfather had been very close to me, they brought back memories of my early years in his home.

About this time, I began to sense some kind of opposition to the success of my ministry that I could not define or identify. Various frustrations produced a cumulative pressure, and I encountered barriers that had never existed before with people close to me. Eventually, I set aside a period for intensive prayer and fasting. Quite soon I began to notice a change in my attitude toward the dragons, and I asked myself, "Who in the Bible is represented as a dragon?" The answer was obvious: Satan (see Revelation 12:1–12).

I then had to ask myself if it was appropriate for a servant of Christ to display in his home objects that typify Christ's adversary,

Satan. Again, the answer was clear: No! I struggled inwardly for a while, but finally I got rid of the dragons as a simple act of obedience.

At that time my income from Bible teaching in the United States was just sufficient to cover my family's basic needs. Shortly after I disposed of the dragons, however, my financial position improved dramatically. My income more than doubled, and a long-delayed legacy came through. I was able to buy a home, which played a decisive part in the extension of my ministry. Nine years later I sold that house for more than three times as much as I paid for it, exactly at a time when God was challenging me to major new financial commitments.

The more I pondered this, the more certain I became that these embroidered dragons had brought a curse into my house. By disposing of them, I had released myself from the curse and opened myself up to the blessing God had planned for me. It gave me new insight into the passage in Deuteronomy 7:25–26, where Moses warned Israel against any association with the idolatrous nations of Canaan: "The images of their gods you are to burn in the fire. Do not covet the silver and gold on them, and do not take it for yourselves, or you will be ensnared by it, for it is detestable to the LORD your God. Do not bring a detestable thing into your house or you, like it, will be set apart for destruction. Utterly abhor and detest it, for it is set apart for destruction." My embroidered dragons were not silver or gold, but they certainly were images of a false god who had been worshiped for millennia in China. By bringing them into my home, I had unknowingly exposed myself—and my family with me—to a curse. How grateful I was to the Holy Spirit for opening my eyes to what was at stake!

A few years later, I met a Jewish lady named Miriam in South Africa who is a believer in Jesus. She personally told me her testimony.

She was a very highly qualified executive secretary, and, influenced by some Christian teaching, she prayed for the best-paid job in her profession in Cape Town. And she got it! She found herself working for a man who was a president of his particular business, and she soon discovered that he and all the executives in the company were in a strange cult led by a prophetess.

After a little while, her boss said to her, "Our guru has pronounced blessings over us, and we would like you to type them out for us." When Miriam started to type, she discovered that they were, in fact, fortune-telling, with occult overtones. As a committed Christian she did not feel free to type them, so her boss graciously exempted her from this task. My guess is that the guru then heard about this incident and prayed some kind of prayer against the secretary. Such a prayer would, of course, be a channel for occult power.

Almost immediately afterwards, Miriam began to develop acute arthritis in both hands. Her fingers curled up and became absolutely stiff and rigid. She could not bend them or work, and the pain was agonizing. She could not even sleep in the same bed with her husband, because every time he moved, the movement of the bed caused intense pain in her fingers. A consultant doctor diagnosed it as rheumatoid arthritis.

A Christian friend of this secretary had heard my three messages, "Curses, Cause and Cure," and brought the cassettes for Miriam to listen to. At the end of the third cassette, I lead people in a prayer of release from the curse over their lives. At that point the cassette jammed. It would not go forward, it would not go back and it would not eject!

The friend who had brought the cassette, however, had a printed version of this prayer of release. Miriam was still quite skeptical and thought that curses only belonged to the Dark Ages. She had listened to the cassettes just to please her friend and only reluctantly agreed to read out this prayer of release. But as she did, her fingers uncurled and became completely free, and the pain ceased. By the time Miriam had finished praying, she was perfectly healed. She then went back to the same doctor, who could find nothing wrong with her.

There was no prayer for healing. There was just a prayer of release from a curse.

Study questions:

1. What was significant about the teenage girl's healing?
2. Why does the author believe that the embroidered dragons brought a curse on his family?
3. What seemed to have brought a curse on Miriam?
4. In each case, what brought release from the curse?
5. Are there any incidents in your own life that seem to show a similar pattern?

2

What Scripture Says

You may be surprised at how much the Bible has to say about blessings and curses. Altogether, words for blessings and curses occur over 600 times. Words for "bless" or "blessing" occur about 410 times, and that is not counting instances where the word in the original text just has the meaning of "happy" or "fortunate" (as, for example, in the Beatitudes). The word *curse*, in various forms, occurs about 230 times. Yet when I began to study this, I could not recall hearing even one message that dealt systematically with the whole subject.

The power of words

Both blessings and curses are usually expressed in words—spoken, written or inwardly uttered. But those are not ordinary words: They are charged with supernatural power. They belong to the invisible, spiritual realm that holds forces that can ultimately shape our destiny, even in the visible realm of day-to-day events. The book of Proverbs has much to say about the power of words:

> Reckless words pierce like a sword,
> but the tongue of the wise brings healing.
>
> Proverbs 12:18

> The tongue that brings healing is a tree of life,
> but a deceitful tongue crushes the spirit.
>
> Proverbs 15:4

> The tongue has the power of life and death,
> and those who love it will eat its fruit.
>
> Proverbs 18:21

James also speaks of the use of words:

> Likewise the tongue is a small part of the body, but it makes great boasts. Consider what a great forest is set on fire by a small spark.

The tongue also is a fire, a world of evil among the parts of the body. It corrupts the whole person, sets the whole course of his life on fire, and is itself set on fire by hell....
With the tongue we praise our Lord and Father, and with it we curse men, who have been made in God's likeness. Out of the same mouth come praise and cursing. My brothers, this should not be.

James 3:5–6, 9–10

James uses vivid imagery to emphasize the tremendous power that words have to affect people and situations, either for good or for evil. It is significant that he singles out both blessings and curses as words that can be charged with this kind of almost unlimited power.

Physical means of blessing and cursing

Words are not, however, the only channels through which the spiritual power of blessings or curses may be transmitted. There are various ways in which, at times, physical objects may become vehicles for this kind of power.

In Exodus 30:22–33, the Lord gave instructions to Moses for making a special oil that was to be used solely for anointing the Tabernacle and its furniture, and also the priests who were to minister in the Tabernacle. In Leviticus 8:1–12 there is an account of how this oil was applied. It concludes, "Then Moses took the anointing oil and anointed the tabernacle and everything in it, and so consecrated them. He sprinkled some of the oil on the altar seven times, anointing the altar and all its utensils and the basin with its stand, to consecrate them. He poured some of the anointing oil on Aaron's head and anointed him to consecrate him" (verses 10–12). The word *consecrate* in this passage means "to set apart to God, to make holy." Thus the anointing oil became a vehicle to impart the blessing of holiness both to the Tabernacle and its furniture and to the priests who ministered in it.

Later in Israel's history, olive oil was used to impart blessing to the kings who were to rule the people on God's behalf. First Samuel 16:13 records how the prophet Samuel set David apart as God's chosen king: "So Samuel took the horn of oil and anointed him in the presence of his brothers, and from that day on the Spirit of the LORD came on David in power." The oil poured on David's head became a vehicle through which the blessing of the Holy Spirit was released to equip him for his task as king.

In the New Testament, the emblems used in the Lord's Supper

likewise become vehicles of God's blessing to those who partake of them. In 1 Corinthians 10:16 Paul says, "Is not the cup of thanksgiving for which we give thanks a participation in the blood of Christ?" The Greek words here translated as "thanksgiving" and "give thanks" can also be translated "blessing" and "bless." For those who partake in faith, the emblems transmit the blessing of God. The cup transmits the blessings of the New Covenant to those who drink from it.

In all the ordinances described above there is no "magic." The blessings are not inherent in the physical objects as such. They are imparted only to those who apprehend the will of God as revealed in Scripture and who by personal faith and obedience receive what is offered to them in the elements. Without faith and obedience, there is no blessing.

On the contrary, in 1 Corinthians 11:29, Paul says concerning the emblems of the Lord's Supper, "For anyone who eats and drinks without recognizing the body of the Lord eats and drinks judgment on himself." Such, then, are the alternatives. Faith and obedience enable us to receive God's blessing; unbelief and disobedience provoke God's judgment. In both cases spiritual power is transmitted through physical objects, whether for blessing or for judgment. In various forms of false religion and the occult, there is virtually no limit to the ways in which objects can become vehicles of curses.

In Exodus 20:4–5, the second of the Ten Commandments explicitly forbids the making of any kind of idol or image for religious purposes and warns that those who break this commandment will bring judgment not only on themselves, but also on at least three following generations: "You shall not make for yourself an idol in the form of anything in heaven above or on the earth beneath or in the waters below. You shall not bow down to them or worship them; for I, the LORD your God, am a jealous God, punishing the children for the sin of the fathers to the third and fourth generation of those who hate me."

I have already described how the embroidered oriental dragons exposed me to the invisible influence of a curse, even though I had no intention of worshiping them. Nevertheless, they represented an object of idolatrous worship for many centuries. Not only were they a barrier that kept me from moving forward into the blessing of prosperity, they even kept me from seeing that the blessing was actually there. Only after I was free from their influence could I discern by faith what God had prepared for me.

Since that time I have observed the same effect in the lives of many people under a curse—it not only keeps them from receiving the blessing God is offering to them, it also keeps them from realizing that the blessing is there to receive. Only when the Holy Spirit shines the light of Scripture into our lives do we begin to understand how the devil has been deceiving and cheating us.

So curses and blessings are words that are charged with supernatural power—maybe the power of God, maybe the power of the devil. They are words that impinge upon people's lives, and to a large extent determine their destiny. Often they will go on from generation to generation, even for thousands of years.

The blessing of Abraham

One of the first biblical examples of blessings is in Genesis 22. Abraham had been willing to offer up his son Isaac in response to the Lord's requirement, and then at the last moment the Lord provided a ram to be offered instead of Isaac. "The angel of the Lord called to Abraham from heaven a second time and said, 'I swear by myself, declares the Lord, that because you have done this and have not withheld your son, your only son, I will surely bless you and make your descendants as numerous as the stars in the sky and as the sand on the seashore'" (Genesis 22:15–17). Notice that the blessing was to continue on to Isaac's descendants, from generation to generation.

Then God continues, "Your descendants will take possession of the cities of their enemies, and through your offspring all nations on earth will be blessed, because you have obeyed me" (verses 17–18). It is very important to notice the reason for the blessing— because Abraham obeyed God's voice. That is the basic reason for the blessing of God in any life.

If you look on a little further in Genesis 27, you find how Isaac blessed his son Jacob. The strange thing is that Isaac thought he was blessing Esau, who was the firstborn. But while Esau was off hunting the venison that Isaac had asked for, Rebekah (Isaac's wife) substituted Jacob, her favorite son. In order to get away with the deception, because Isaac was blind, she dressed Jacob up in Esau's clothes and cooked a young goat instead of the venison. Then she served it the way her husband liked it and wrapped the goat's skin around Jacob's neck and arms, so that he would seem hairy like his brother Esau.

Along came Jacob, pretending to be Esau, and when Isaac checked, saying, "Are you my son Esau?" Jacob lied, saying, "Yes, I am"! Then Isaac asked for the food that had been prepared. We have to acknowledge that Isaac was somewhat carnal. He wanted his stomach filled with his favorite food before he could pronounce his blessing!

> Jacob brought it to him and he ate; and he brought some wine and he drank. Then his father Isaac said to him, "Come here, my son, and kiss me."
> So he went to him and kissed him. When Isaac caught the smell of his clothes, he blessed him and said,
>
> "Ah, the smell of my son
>   is like the smell of a field
>   that the LORD has blessed.
> May God give you of heaven's dew
>   and of earth's richness—
>   an abundance of grain and new wine.
> May nations serve you
>   and peoples bow down to you.
> Be lord over your brothers,
>   and may the sons of your mother bow down to you.
> May those who curse you be cursed
>   and those who bless you be blessed."
>
> Genesis 27:25–29

Isaac's blessing was tremendous in its scope, and it was to continue on from generation to generation.

Now a little while later, Esau came in with the venison and tried to offer it to his father. Isaac then realized that he had been deceived and that he had blessed Jacob when he thought he was blessing Esau. But note Isaac's reaction: "Isaac trembled violently and said, 'Who was it, then, that hunted game and brought it to me? I ate it just before you came and I blessed him—and indeed he will be blessed!'" (Genesis 27:33). Isn't that amazing? Isaac had thought he was blessing Esau, but he knew the words that he had spoken had been supernaturally given him from God. For this reason he could not "unsay" it.

A blessing like this is supernatural. It is not mere wishful thinking or the expression of human sentiment. It is something supernaturally empowered that determines the destiny of the one who receives it and of succeeding generations. That is true of blessings and curses alike.

Study questions:

1. What does Scripture say about the power of words?
2. By what other means can blessings and curses be imparted?
3. How does the Lord's Supper transmit a blessing?
4. What is the basic reason for God's blessing, as shown in the story of Abraham?
5. What does Isaac's blessing tell us about the nature of blessings and curses?

3

Moses' List of Blessings and Curses

Some people accept the fact that blessings are real but are skeptical about curses, which they associate with superstitious medieval practices. Yet we cannot focus exclusively on one aspect of opposites because it is acceptable to us and simply ignore the other. The opposite of hot is cold; both are real. The opposite of good is evil; both are real. In just the same way, blessings are real and so are curses.

My ministry brings me in touch with Christians from many different backgrounds in many different lands. I find that most of God's people do not know how to discern between blessings and curses, or to recognize them. Many Christians who should be enjoying blessings are actually enduring curses because they do not understand the basis on which they can be released.

God is the sole and supreme source of all blessings, although they may come to us through many channels. Curses, too, often proceed from God, but He is not the sole source. The curses that proceed from God are one of His main ways of bringing judgment on the rebellious, the unbelieving and the ungodly. The history of the human race provides a long, sad record of the outworking of such curses.

In Deuteronomy 27 God ordained that when the Israelites came into their Promised Land, they were to pronounce upon themselves twelve curses if they disobeyed God in certain respects. "On the same day Moses commanded the people: When you have crossed the Jordan, these tribes shall stand on Mount Gerizim to bless the people: Simeon, Levi, Judah, Issachar, Joseph and Benjamin. And these tribes shall stand on Mount Ebal to pronounce curses: Reuben, Gad, Asher, Zebulun, Dan and Naphtali" (Deuteronomy 27:11–13). They could not enter into the Promised Land without being exposed either to a blessing, if they were obedient, or to a curse, if they were disobedient. There was no way into the Promised Land but through blessings and curses.

It has become fashionable to suggest that the Old Testament depicts a God of wrath and judgment, while the New Testament depicts a God of love and mercy. In fact, the two Testaments are consistent with each other. They both depict God as being, at the same time, a God of mercy and judgment.

The story of Jericho, related in Joshua 6, combines these two sides of God's dealings vividly and dramatically. While the city perished under the comprehensive judgment of God, the harlot Rahab emerged unscathed with her entire family. Furthermore, Rahab became the wife of Salmon, one of the princes of Judah, and took her place in the genealogical line from which Israel's Messiah, Jesus, was to come! (See Matthew 1:5.)

In Romans 1:17–18 Paul explains that the Gospel contains the supreme revelation of these two aspects of God, His mercy and His judgment: "For in the gospel a righteousness from God is revealed, a righteousness that is by faith from first to last.... The wrath of God is being revealed from heaven against all the godlessness and wickedness of men." Jesus' sacrifice makes the righteousness of God mercifully available to all who receive it by faith. Yet it is also the ultimate revelation of God's wrath, poured out upon Jesus when He became identified with human sin. Christians who question the reality of God's judgment on sin should ponder afresh the significance of the crucifixion. Even Jesus could not make sin acceptable to God, but had to endure its punishment.

In Romans 11:22 Paul presents these two aspects of God's dealings side by side: "Consider therefore the kindness and sternness of God." To obtain an accurate picture of God, we must always keep both aspects of His character before us. His blessings proceed out of His kindness, but His judgments proceed out of His sternness. Both are equally real.

Hearing and obeying God's voice

The 68 verses of Deuteronomy 28 are devoted solely to the theme of blessings and curses. In verses 1 and 2, Moses speaks first of blessings: "If you fully obey the LORD your God and carefully follow all his commands that I give you today, ... All these blessings will come upon you and accompany you." The first part could be more literally translated, "If you will listen, listening to the voice of the LORD your God,..." The repetition of the verb *to listen* gives it added emphasis. The conditions for enjoying the blessings are, first, listening to God's voice and, second, doing what He says.

Under the New Covenant, in John 10:27, Jesus described those whom He acknowledged as His "sheep"—that is, His true disciples: "My sheep listen to my voice ... and they follow me." The requirements are still the same: recognizing the Lord's voice and following Him in obedience. That is the basis on which God blessed Abraham. He said, "All these blessings shall come upon you because you have obeyed my voice" (Genesis 22:18). You do not need to go running after the blessings. When you meet the conditions, God will take care of the blessings.

Nothing is more unique and distinctive than a person's voice. Hearing the Lord's voice takes us beyond mere religious observances. It implies an intimate relationship with Him in which He can speak to each one of us personally.

The Lord does not usually speak to our physical ears or to our natural minds. His communication is Spirit-to-spirit—that is, by His Spirit to our spirits. His voice penetrates to the innermost depths of our being, and from there its vibrations are felt in every area of our personalities.

The Lord may speak in this way through the Bible, or He may impart a word of direct revelation. Merely reading the Bible, however, is not sufficient by itself, unless the words on its pages are transformed by the Holy Spirit into a living voice.

In Deuteronomy 28:15, Moses states the primary cause of all curses: "If you do not obey the LORD your God and do not carefully follow all his commands and decrees I am giving you today, all these curses will come upon you and overtake you." The cause of curses is exactly opposite to that of blessings. Blessings result from listening to God's voice and doing what He says. Curses result from not listening to God's voice and not doing what He says. This refusal to hear and obey God's voice can be summed up in one word: rebellion.

Summary of the blessings

It is well worth studying the whole of Deuteronomy 28 to understand this subject. But this is the basic list of blessings in the chapter:

- Exaltation—being lifted up high
- Health
- Fertility
- Prosperity
- Victory
- God's favor

This passage describes a condition in which every area of a person's life is fruitful and reproductive, including family, livestock, crops, business and the exercise of creative talents. All of these should reflect God's blessing in appropriate ways.

In his list of curses in verses 16–68, Moses goes into much greater detail than with the blessings. Essentially, however, they are the opposite of blessings.

Summary of the curses

- Humiliation
- Inability to reproduce in any area of your life
- Mental and physical sickness
- Family breakdowns
- Poverty
- Defeat
- Oppression
- Failure
- God's disfavor

Earlier, in verse 13, Moses says, "The LORD will make you the head, not the tail." The head makes the decisions; the tail gets dragged around. The head takes initiative, exercises self-control, makes appropriate decisions and sees them successfully carried out. The tail is dragged around by forces and circumstances it does not understand and cannot control.

Moses adds, "You will always be at the top, never at the bottom" (verse 13). This determines whether you are struggling "under the circumstances" or above them.

Which end are you, the head or the tail? Are you making the decisions? Are you taking the initiative? Are you determining the way things happen? Or are you at the mercy of circumstances, under financial pressure, health pressure or family pressure, and just being dragged around? If you are the tail, it is a curse; if you are the head, it is a blessing.

Study questions:

1. How are the Old and New Testaments consistent in revealing both the judgment and the mercy of God?
2. What is the primary cause of blessings, and the primary cause of curses?
3. How does Deuteronomy 28 summarize the blessings?
4. How does Deuteronomy 28 summarize the curses?
5. Are you the head or the tail—struggling under the circumstances or triumphing over them?

4

Seven Indications of a Curse

Through personal observation and experience, I compiled the following list of seven problems that indicate that a curse is at work. When I compared my list with that of Moses in Deuteronomy 28, I saw a close correspondence between them.

Mental and emotional breakdown

The corresponding phrases from Deuteronomy 28 are "madness," "confusion," "an anxious mind," "a despairing heart," "constant suspense," "dread" and "terror" (verses 20, 28, 65, 66, 67). The mind and the heart—the inner citadel of human personality—have been breached by invading, hostile forces. Such people no longer have full control over their own thoughts and emotions and reactions. They may be "haunted" by an inner voice taunting them: "You're losing control ... there's no hope for you ... your mother ended up in a mental institution, and you'll be next!"

I have been amazed to discover how many Christians are going through these inner struggles. Often they are reluctant to acknowledge their problem to others, or even to themselves, for fear this would be a denial of their faith. Two key words are *confusion* and *depression*—they often indicate that someone is struggling under a curse.

Repeated or chronic illness

Deuteronomy 28 mentions numerous conditions including "wasting disease," "fever and inflammation," "blight," "tumors, festering sores, and the itch, from which you cannot be cured," "painful boils," "fearful plagues ... severe and lingering illnesses" and "every kind of sickness" (verses 22, 27, 35, 59, 61). This list does not necessarily indicate that every form of sickness and disease is the direct result of a curse. However, key words like *incurable, extraordinary, dreaded, prolonged* and *lingering* are warning signals. A lack of clear medical diagnosis, especially when these things run in families, would often indicate the presence of a curse.

A friend of mine, who is a pastor, was diagnosed at the age of sixty with hemochromatosis, a disease that causes the patient to produce too much iron in the blood and store it in the vital organs. His father had died of the same disease at 65. The doctor pronounced it hereditary, incurable and life threatening.

After much prayer, my friend stood before his congregation in a Sunday morning service and made a simple, unemotional affirmation: "In the name of Jesus, I release myself from any evil inheritance from my father." He was immediately and completely cured. Five years have passed and there has been no recurrence of the problem.

In all these cases, even when we strongly suspect that a curse is at work, we must rely on the Holy Spirit for discernment.

Barrenness, repeated miscarriages and related female problems

The key phrase here from Deuteronomy 28:18 is, "The fruit of your womb will be cursed." This curse may affect any of the various reproductive organs or functions. The category of "female problems" includes the inability to conceive, a tendency to miscarry, failure to menstruate, irregular menstruation, debilitating menstrual cramps, "frigidity," cysts, tumors or other growths or structural defects affecting the reproductive organs. Often all the women in a family may be afflicted with problems of this kind.

Before we minister to such women, we first instruct them on the nature and causes of curses and then pray with them for release. Often this has produced wholeness in the affected areas, even without specific prayer for healing.

At a meeting in Amsterdam in July 1985, a couple who had been married for twelve years without being able to have children came for prayer. My second wife, Ruth, laid hands on the woman's womb and spoke that she would be "neither barren nor unfruitful." The whole congregation was asked to stand and join them in prayer, and the husband and wife both felt strongly that the Lord had heard their prayers. Two years later at a meeting in England, the couple came and showed us a beautiful baby boy, the manifestation of the blessing that replaced the curse of barrenness over their lives.

Marriage breakdown and alienation in families

One effect of the curse in this area is described in Deuteronomy 28:41: "You will have sons and daughters but you will not keep them, because they will go into captivity." Countless parents in the present generation have experienced this curse. They have seen their sons and daughters taken captive by a rebellious subculture devoted to drugs, drunkenness, promiscuous sex, satanic music and every form of the occult. Wherever that power goes to work, it will ultimately break up the family.

The word *alienation* describes the force that comes between husbands and wives, parents and children, brothers and sisters and all others who should be united by the bonds of family. The enemy's goal is the destruction of the family.

Continuing financial or material insufficiency

Two related phrases in Deuteronomy 28 are, "Your basket and your kneading trough will be cursed" (verse 17), and "You will be unsuccessful in everything you do" (verse 29). Even more graphic, however, are verses 47–48: "Because you did not serve the LORD your God joyfully and gladly in the time of prosperity, therefore in hunger and thirst, in nakedness and dire poverty, you will serve the enemies the LORD sends against you."

Many people experience a temporary financial shortage at some point in their lives. When insufficiency becomes a chronic condition, however, oppressing and enslaving, and when the best-intentioned efforts yield no solution, then that almost certainly indicates a curse at work. Certainly, God has great compassion on the poor, and Christians should also be compassionate and sacrificial on behalf of the poor. But Scripture never suggests that God inflicts poverty as a blessing upon His believing people.

In 2 Corinthians 9:8, Paul says, "And God is able to make all grace abound to you, so that in all things at all times, having all that you need, you will abound in every good work." Paul doubles and redoubles his words to emphasize the generosity of God's provision for His people. This provision transcends mere sufficiency and lifts us to a level of abundance where we have something over and above our own needs to minister to the needs of others.

It would be unscriptural to interpret poverty and abundance by the materialistic standards of contemporary Western civilization. God's riches are provided for us, not to squander on carnal self-indulgence, but for every good work—that is, sharing with others the blessings of grace that have enriched our own lives. The greater the gap between what you need to do God's will in your life and what you have, the greater the degree of poverty.

Faith to appropriate God's abundance is certain to be tested. There may be times when we have to content ourselves with the barest sufficiency. Once our motives have been purified and our faith has stood the test, however, God releases His abundance in the measure that He can trust us to use for His glory.

There is also a higher level of wealth than just the material. When Moses turned his back on the luxury of Egypt and settled in a remote desert region, the writer of Hebrews says that he "regarded disgrace for the sake of Christ as of greater value than the treasures of Egypt, because he was looking ahead to his reward" (11:26). Moses exchanged material wealth for riches of a higher order.

Some Christians deliberately renounce material wealth in order to identify with the poor and oppressed of the earth, while others endure affliction and persecution for Christ's sake. They may be deprived of everything that could be described as material wealth, but instead they are heirs to spiritual wealth. Nevertheless, the basic principle is that prosperity is a blessing, while persistent poverty is a curse.

Being "accident-prone"

This phrase describes a person who is unnaturally prone to accidents. Perhaps it is hinted at in this phrase in Deuteronomy 28:29: "At midday you will grope about like a blind man in the dark." One characteristic of this curse might be seen in what are called "freak" accidents. Some people are good drivers, yet they have an abnormally high number of car accidents, perhaps often "the other person's fault." Such people would typically comment, "Why does it always happen to me?"

It almost seems that there is an invisible, malicious force working against accident-prone people. At critical moments, they trip up or make rash, unpremeditated moves. It is statistically recognized. Some insurance companies use this kind of analysis to identify people who would be unusually high risks and set their premiums accordingly!

A history of suicides or unnatural deaths

The references to unnatural or untimely death in Deuteronomy 28 are too numerous to mention. A curse that takes this form affects not just a single individual but a larger social unit, such as a family or tribe, and normally continues from one generation to another. The ancient Greeks recognized this force and gave it the status of a "goddess," whom they named "Nemesis." A very conspicuous family that bears all the marks of this curse is the Kennedy family.

Quite often people who are affected by this type of curse experience a strong foreboding. They sense something dark and evil in the road ahead, but they do not know how to avoid it. Some set dates for their own deaths: "I know I'll never live to see 45." They have a kind of negative faith that unconsciously invites evil spirits to take them over. In John 8:44 Jesus warned us that Satan is a murderer. The spirit of death can drive a person to suicide or other untimely death.

Study questions:

1. How does mental or physical health link with blessings and curses?
2. Do you think a curse on families is evident in our culture?
3. What is the biblical perspective on wealth and poverty?
4. How might being accident-prone or having a family history of suicides and unnatural deaths indicate a curse?
5. Are any of these indications of curses present in your personal or family life?

5

No Curse without a Cause

The operation of blessings and curses in our lives is not haphazard or unpredictable. On the contrary, the Bible shows that both operate according to eternal, unchanging laws.

In Proverbs 26:2 Solomon makes it clear that there is a reason for every curse: "Like a fluttering sparrow or a darting swallow, an undeserved curse does not come to rest." This principle has a double application. A curse cannot take effect unless there is a cause for it. On the other hand, wherever there is a curse at work, a cause can be found. I have learned by experience that discovering that cause can help people to obtain release.

This section lays bare the causes of the main curses that commonly afflict our lives. After reading it, you will be better equipped to understand them and to apply God's remedy.

Idolatry and false gods

The form of disobedience that most surely and inevitably provokes God's curse is the breaking of the first two of the Ten Commandments. These are stated in Exodus 20:1–5:

> And God spoke all these words: "I am the LORD your God, who brought you out of Egypt, out of the land of slavery.
> You shall have no other gods before me.
> You shall not make yourself an idol in the form of anything in heaven above or on the earth beneath or in the waters below. You shall not bow down to them or worship them; for I, the LORD your God, am a jealous God, punishing the children for the sin of the fathers to the third and fourth generation of those who hate me."

In Romans 1:22–23 Paul speaks of people whose hearts are "darkened": "Although they claimed to be wise, they became fools and exchanged the glory of the immortal God for images made to look like mortal man and birds and animals and reptiles." God's judgment on the breaking of these first two commandments bears the characteristic mark of a curse: It continues from generation to generation. In some nations and cultures, the practice of worshiping false gods goes back over hundreds and even thousands of years, compounding the effect many times over. The curse on a person from such a background is like a deeply rooted weed. Such a "weed" has a long tap root representing the influences of ancestors, as well as weaker lateral roots representing sin in the person's own lifetime.

Before any person can enjoy true liberty and the fullness of the new creation in Christ, this weed must be completely uprooted. Nothing but the supernatural grace and power of God can effectively remove all these roots. But thank God, there is hope in the promise of Jesus (Matthew 15:13): "Every plant that my heavenly Father has not planted will be pulled up by the roots." The sins that bring this generational curse, however, do not stop short at the more obvious forms of idolatry. They include other practices that may not be openly idolatrous or even religious (see chapter 9 for more details).

There are actually only two sources of supernatural knowledge and power in the universe: either God or Satan. Every form of supernatural knowledge or power that does not proceed from God, therefore, necessarily proceeds from Satan. One is legitimate and the other is illegitimate.

Since God's Kingdom is the Kingdom of light, His servants know whom they are serving and what they are doing. On the other hand, since Satan's kingdom is a kingdom of darkness, most of those in his kingdom do not know the true identity of the one whom they are serving or the true nature of what they are doing.

It was this craving for illegitimate knowledge that prompted the first human transgression in the Garden of Eden. God had set an invisible boundary between Adam and Eve and the tree of the knowledge of good and evil. As soon as this boundary was crossed, they found themselves in Satan's territory and came under a curse.

Those who still trespass in occult areas are seeking from Satan the supernatural knowledge or power that God does not permit us to seek from any other source but Him. In so doing, they are acknowledging Satan as a god besides the one true God, thus breaking the first of the Ten Commandments. Therefore, all who are involved in the occult expose themselves to a curse, extending even to the fourth generation.

Injustice to the weak and helpless

Deuteronomy 27 condemns oppression and injustice, especially against the weak and helpless. There are certainly many examples of such behavior in our contemporary culture, but I believe the one most likely to provoke God's curse is the deliberate aborting of an unborn infant.

How strange that some people who are rightly fighting against racial prejudice and injustice actually condone and promote the practice of abortion. Some who would never think of raising a hand in violence against a small child feel no compassion toward an even smaller child in the womb. God classes abortion as murder, and around the world millions of lives are being blighted by the curse that follows this act.

Native Americans in the United States placed a curse on the White House because the American government regularly broke its treaties with their ancestors. Believe me, Native Americans know how to curse! From 1860 to 1980 every president elected in the twentieth year died in office. I relate this to two things: the government's betrayal of the vulnerable Native Americans and the fact that Abraham Lincoln, the president elected in 1860, permitted a spiritist séance to be conducted in the White House by his wife, who later ended up in a mental institution.

I believe that the same would have happened to Ronald Reagan, who was elected president in 1980. Just before he took the presidential oath, a large group of Christians prayed to release not just Reagan, but the presidency, from this curse. In fact, an attempt was made on his life early in his presidency. The bullet lodged within one inch of his heart, but his life was spared. I believe this was God's vindication of the prayer that released the curse.

Once again, we see that curses affect not only individuals, but nations. Isaiah 58:6–12 clearly teaches that as we work to break the chains of injustice and minister to the poor and needy, we will receive the answer to our own prayers and also release blessing in our communities.

Wrong sexual practices

Sadly, some Christians believe that sex is somehow unclean and to be ashamed of. The Bible, however, shows that it is something sacred and beautiful, and part of the Creator's original plan for humanity. For this reason, God has set stringent boundaries around the sexual act to protect it from abuse and perversion, and these are set out in Deuteronomy 27:20–23.

Any form of unnatural sex brings a curse. This includes incestuous relationships with family members and bestiality (sex with animals). Tragically, today we must acknowledge that millions of children are sexually victimized by their fathers or other relatives. The Bible also forbids all expressions of homosexuality. Leviticus 18:22 says, "Do not lie with a man as one lies with a woman; that is detestable." The word *detestable* is also used in Deuteronomy 18 to describe occult practices.

Today, many of the boundaries designed to protect the sanctity of sex are being deliberately set aside, sometimes even in the name of Christianity. Promiscuity is extremely common, and the boundaries of marriage are not respected. Yet no arguments based on situational ethics can alter the laws of God that govern human behavior. All who indulge in sexual perversion or immorality expose themselves to serious consequences.

Anti-Semitism

God called our forefather Abraham (when he was still called Abram) to go out from his city, Ur of the Chaldees, to an unknown destiny.

> The LORD had said to Abram, "Leave your country, your people and your father's household and go to the land I will show you.
>
> I will make you into a great nation
> and I will bless you;
> I will make your name great,
> and you will be a blessing.
> I will bless those who bless you,
> and whoever curses you I will curse;
> and all peoples on earth
> will be blessed through you."
>
> Genesis 12:1–3

This call is rich in blessing, but there is a curse, too. When God calls a person to a special task, he or she automatically becomes also a target for Satan's special enmity. Therefore, God built into Abraham's call a special protective clause: "Whoever curses you I will curse."

Later on in the Bible this protection is specifically extended through Isaac to Jacob (Genesis 27:29) and then to the whole nation of Israel (Numbers 24:9). So God has pronounced a curse on all who curse the Jewish people.

Throughout many centuries the professing Christian Church has often been guilty of propagating flagrant anti-Semitism. Yet the Church owes every spiritual blessing to the Jewish people: Without them, we would have no apostles, no Bible and no Savior. Each of us needs to examine whether we or any of our ancestors have been enemies of the Jewish people. When we repent of the sin of anti-Semitism, the dark shadow of that curse will lift from major sections of the Church and be replaced by God's blessing.

Legalism and carnality

A completely different example of a curse is found in Jeremiah 17:5–6: "This is what the Lord says: 'Cursed is the one who trusts in man, who depends on flesh for his strength and whose heart turns away from the Lord.'" The word *flesh* here refers not to the physical body, but to the fallen nature we have all inherited from Adam. His desire was not so much to do evil as to be independent from God, and this desire is at work in all his descendants.

Although this is true for individuals, it applies especially to Christian churches that have tasted the grace of God but then have turned away and begun trusting in their own efforts, their own intelligence, their own methods and their own religious forms. They have armed themselves with human strength. The blessing of God has gone, and in its place a curse has come over their congregations.

Almost every significant movement in Christendom originated in a powerful, supernatural work of God's Spirit. Yet most of these movements no longer emphasize the grace and power of God. While they may have achieved religious and intellectual respectability, they have forfeited God's favor.

Putting human ability and material resources in the place of divine grace exalts the carnal over the spiritual. Often theology is exalted above revelation, academic achievement above character, psychology over discernment, programs over the leading of the Holy Spirit, eloquence above supernatural power, human reason above the walk of faith, musical talent above true worship and laws above love.

Paul struggled with legalism in the church of Galatia, crying, "You foolish Galatians! ... After beginning with the Spirit, are you now trying to attain your goal by human effort? . . . All who rely on observing the law are under a curse" (Galatians 3:1, 3, 10). Cut off from the source of grace, Christians can degenerate not only into legalism, but also carnality. These are works of the flesh, or the sinful nature. Some are listed in Galatians 5:19–21, including sexual immorality and impurity, hatred, jealousy, fits of rage, selfish ambition, dissensions, factions, envy, drunkenness and orgies. Yet in the final analysis, legalism is as deadly as any of these.

Stealing, perjury and robbing God

The prophet Zechariah had a vision of a scroll that contained curses on both sides. One cursed thieves, and the other cursed people who lied and swore falsely (committed perjury) in the name of the Lord. Whenever this curse applied, the entire house of the person was destroyed.

Many houses are destroyed and many families are broken up because a curse has come in. Who can calculate how many people must be under a curse if we include all those who steal or perjure themselves? Many are not honest in their tax returns—that could bring a curse on them. In the United States it would include a lot of people, many of them churchgoers.

Haggai spoke the word of the Lord about the blight that was affecting the lives of his people: " 'Is it a time for you yourselves to be living in your paneled houses, while this house remains a ruin?' Now this is what the LORD Almighty says: 'Give careful thought to your ways. You have planted much, but have harvested little. You eat, but never have enough. You drink, but never have your fill. You put on clothes, but are not warm. You earn wages, only to put them in a purse with holes in it. . . . Why? . . . Because of my house, which remains a ruin, while each of you is busy with his own house' " (Haggai 1:3–5, 9). The Israelites should have had everything they required to satisfy their main material needs, yet there was always a deficiency. Haggai stated that the invisible force eroding their provisions was a curse they had brought upon themselves by putting their own selfish concerns before the needs of God's house.

In affluent countries, although many people are earning far more than their parents or grandparents ever earned and have far more luxuries, they are plagued with a restless craving that is never satisfied. In many nations, the level of personal debt is higher than ever before.

Through the prophet Malachi, God accuses His people of theft in its most serious form: "Will a man rob God? Yet you rob me. But you ask, 'How do we rob you?' In tithes and offerings. You are under a curse—the whole nation of you—because you are robbing me" (Malachi 3:8–9). Yet God instructs His people how to pass out from under the curse and enter into His blessing: "'Bring the whole tithe into the storehouse, that there may be food in my house. Test me in this,' says the Lord Almighty, 'and see if I will not throw open the floodgates of heaven and pour out so much blessing that you will not have room enough for it. I will prevent pests from devouring your crops, and the vines in your fields will not cast their fruit. . . . Then all the nations will call you blessed, for yours will be a delightful land'" (Malachi 3:10–12).

To repent from robbery, whether it is from God or human beings, restitution is required. In the New Testament, the covenant of grace operates not through external laws about tithing, but through what the Spirit of God has written on believers' hearts. In 2 Corinthians 9:7, Paul says, "Each man should give what he has decided in his heart to give, not reluctantly or under compulsion, for God loves a cheerful giver." One thing is certain: Stinginess toward God provokes His curse, but liberality releases His blessing. A hallmark of the Holy Spirit is generosity, because God Himself is the greatest of all givers.

Study questions:

1. What happens to a curse without a cause?
2. Which forms of disobedience most inevitably provoke God's curse?
3. What is a generational curse? Give an example of a curse affecting nations.
4. Why does legalism bring a curse?
5. What causes of curses may be present in your own life?

6

Blessings and Curses through Authority Figures

Both blessings and curses are part of a vast, invisible, spiritual realm that affects the lives of all of us. One central and decisive factor in this realm is authority. Without understanding this, it is impossible to function effectively in the realm of the spirit.

The principles that govern the exercise of authority are as objective and universal as the law of gravity. A person in an attitude of revolt or denial may decide to reject the law of gravity and jump out of a tenth-floor window. But his rejection of that law in no way invalidates it—he will still fall to his death on the sidewalk below. In the same way, people may ignore or reject the laws of authority, but their lives will still be determined by them.

God the Creator is the supreme source of authority, but He delegates this authority to those He chooses. He placed His authority in the hands of Jesus, who in turn delegates it to others. It may be pictured as an extremely strong cable descending from God the Father to Jesus. In the hands of Jesus, this cable is separated into countless smaller cables that reach to those whom He has appointed—both angelic and human—in various parts of the universe.

In human social relationships, the husband/father is the primary example of a person appointed to exercise authority. However, there are many other commonly recognized authority figures: a ruler over people, a military commander over soldiers, a teacher over students, a pastor over congregational members. We may object to this, but it is true.

God alone has absolute authority. All other forms of authority are limited in some way and valid only within a given sphere. There are also cases where two forms of authority overlap, giving rise to conflicts. Yet it must not be assumed that whenever authority is abused, it is automatically canceled.

A person may exercise authority by blessing those under his or her authority. Genesis 27 records the tremendous importance that both Jacob and Esau attached to the blessing of their father, Isaac, and with good reason, since it determined the history of their descendants. All through the Bible, the blessing of a father is considered second in importance only to that of God Himself.

A person in authority can also curse. One dramatic example is provided in Genesis 31, which records how Jacob and his large family departed by stealth from his uncle Laban's home. Laban pursued and overtook Jacob, accusing him of stealing his teraphim (household images, or gods, used for divination and supposed to protect a home from evil forces). Jacob did not realize that his beloved wife, Rachel, had secretly taken the images, so he reacted indignantly. Protesting his innocence, he added a curse: "If you find anyone who has your gods, he shall not live" (Genesis 31:32). Of course, by taking possession of false gods, Rachel had trespassed in the area of idolatry. She had forfeited God's protection and exposed herself to the curse that follows occult involvement. Rachel succeeded in keeping the teraphim hidden, but the words of Jacob's unwitting curse were charged with authority, equivalent to a sentence of death. The fact that Jacob did not realize that his words were directed against Rachel did not prevent the curse from taking effect. Shortly afterwards Rachel died in labor giving birth to her second son. Such is the authority of the husband to bless or to curse!

In God's plan for marriage, husband and wife become "one flesh," and the authority is shared jointly. Husbands may fail to do this and become arbitrary or despotic. More commonly these days, husbands renege on their responsibilities, leaving the wives to carry burdens of authority that they should have carried together.

If a father's blessing is greatly to be sought, one of the things to be feared most is his curse. In our culture, it is not uncommon for a husband or father to deliberately or carelessly inflict bitter and crushing words against his wife and children. He may say to one child repeatedly, "You'll always be useless." The child's life is then blighted by the negative, destructive words.

In another situation, a man may close bitter arguments with the words, "I hate your guts!" In the following years, his wife requires surgery in her abdomen for various unrelated conditions. Such words are like barbed arrows, tipped with poison. They are difficult to remove, but if left in, they cause even more trouble.

Mothers, too, can inflict curses through wounding words and

controlling attitudes. Teachers can also speak words that blight the future lives of their pupils, often summed up in one brief phrase: "You'll never succeed!" This is very close to the words of the curse in Deuteronomy 28:29: "You will be unsuccessful in everything you do." Whenever I hear such comments, I am on my guard about the possibility that a curse is being uttered.

✗ Our own responses to authority figures, including parents, can bring or perpetuate a curse on us. Remember that the first commandment with a promise of blessing says, "Honor your father and your mother, so that you may live long in the land the LORD your God is giving you" (Exodus 20:12).

Dishonoring parents automatically exposes you to a curse. This does not mean you have to agree with your parents or even do everything they tell you to do—that depends on the way they are living. You may disagree strongly with them yet maintain a respectful attitude.

I have met many people whose lives have been straightened out when they straightened out their attitude toward their parents. In my book *God Is a Matchmaker*, I wrote of one man who was convicted of a lifetime of bitterness and hatred toward his deceased father. He journeyed hundreds of miles to the cemetery where his father was buried, and kneeling beside the grave, poured out his heart to God in deep contrition and repentance. He did not rise from his knees until he knew his sin was forgiven and he was released from its evil effects. From that point on, the whole course of his life changed for the better.

The words of religious leaders have a potential for good or evil that corresponds with the authority of their office. For many centuries in Europe, one main weapon used by the Roman Catholic popes was the papal "ban" (that is, curse), proclaimed on all whom they deemed to be heretics. The effects of these bans can be clearly seen in European history: Some rulers of nations feared a ban more than an actual declaration of war.

But even leaders of little, independent churches with a handful of members can speak words that amount to curses on their members. Sometimes it happens that a pastor clashes with a member of his congregation and the person leaves, maybe in a bad spirit. Out of insecurity, fear or arrogance, the pastor says, "God put you here. If you leave, you'll never prosper." If you break away from some religious groups (not necessarily Christian), they will automatically put a curse upon you. Believe me, that is not something of little consequence. It is real.

The effects of blessings and curses are seldom limited to the individual. They may extend to families, tribes, communities or whole nations. And once they are released, they often continue from generation to generation to generation. This means that a person who is experiencing either a blessing or a curse may not easily discern where it comes from, because it may be in the past, even hundreds of years ago.

I was teaching on this in Adelaide, Australia, and a woman wrote me a letter afterwards. Her ancestors were from Scotland, from a clan called Nyxxon. She gave me historical evidence that because of clan wars between the Scots and the English in the sixteenth century, a bishop of the Church of Scotland had put a curse on that clan. She realized that four centuries later things were still happening in her family because of that curse.

Study questions:

1. Why must we understand the significance of authority in the spiritual realm?
2. What is the importance of the father's curse or blessing?
3. Explain how Jacob inadvertently brought a curse of death upon Rachel, and how she made herself vulnerable to it.
4. Give examples of other authority figures who may bless or curse.
5. What curses or blessings have you received through authority figures? Have you yourself cursed or blessed others?

7

Legitimate Curses
from Servants of God

Curses can legitimately proceed from people representing God. Consider Joshua, who pronounced a curse on anybody who would rebuild Jericho after the children of Israel miraculously recaptured the city.

> At that time Joshua pronounced this solemn oath: "Cursed before the LORD is the man who undertakes to rebuild this city, Jericho:
>
> At the cost of his firstborn son
>   will he lay its foundations;
> at the cost of his youngest
>   will he set up its gates."
>
> Joshua 6:26

That curse was pronounced about 1300 B.C. In about 800 B.C. a man rebuilt Jericho, and we read about it in 1 Kings 16:34. "In Ahab's time, Hiel of Bethel rebuilt Jericho. He laid its foundations at the cost of his firstborn son Abiram, and he set up its gates at the cost of his youngest son Segub, in accordance with the word of the LORD spoken by Joshua son of Nun." Five hundred years later the curse pronounced by Joshua was worked out in that man who rebuilt the city. It cost him two of his children. Can you imagine the doctors of that day trying to determine the cause of their deaths? There may have been no obvious medical reason, and yet they died. The doctors did not know that the cause went back five hundred years to a curse that had been pronounced as a judgment on the city, which God determined should never be rebuilt. Can you see that you may be dealing with things in your life, the cause of which can go back hundreds of years?

Another example is David's song after the deaths of Saul and Jonathan. At various times David pronounced some awe-inspiring curses, many of which are recorded in the Psalms. Just to read them could make one's blood run cold. Yet the role of the man or woman of God is not only to bless, but also to curse.

This is what David said in his lament for Saul and Jonathan: "O mountains of Gilboa, may you have neither dew nor rain, nor fields that yield offerings of grain. For there the shield of the mighty was defiled, the shield of Saul" (2 Samuel 1:21). Does it seem strange to talk to mountains? Those words of David were spoken about a thousand years before Christ. Yet now—nearly three thousand years later—you can go to the mountains of Gilboa and there is still no green vegetation on them. Trees and vegetation will grow on the other mountains all around. The government of Israel works tirelessly to reforest the country and tried to plant trees on that mountain, but they would not grow! The physical evidence of David's words remains.

You will remember that the prophet Elisha had a servant named Gehazi who disobeyed Elisha and ran after Naaman after he had been miraculously healed. Gehazi asked for money and clothing and hid it from Elisha. When he came back, Elisha said, "Was not my spirit with you?" (1 Kings 5:26). Then he said this: "Naaman's leprosy will cling to you and to your descendants forever" (verse 27). And Gehazi went away white with leprosy. What was that the result of? A curse pronounced by a man of God.

In the gospels we read of Jesus cursing the fig tree: "The next day as they were leaving Bethany, Jesus was hungry. Seeing in the distance a fig tree in leaf, he went to find out if it had any fruit. When he reached it, he found nothing but leaves, because it was not the season for figs" (Mark 11:12–13). Many commentators see this fig tree as a symbol of the way the practice of the law had degenerated. It was full of "leaves"—that is, the outward forms of religion—but it did not yield the true fruit of the law, which Jesus summed up as "justice, mercy and faithfulness" (Matthew 23:23). As a result, sincere seekers who looked to that form of religion to satisfy their spiritual hunger were turned away, empty and disappointed.

Knowing that the tree was fruitless, Jesus spoke to the tree, saying, "May no one ever eat fruit from you again" (Mark 11:14). The disciples heard this. Perhaps they thought, "Our Master has gone too far this time!" But in verse 20 we read, "In the morning, as they went along, they saw the fig tree withered from the roots. Peter remembered and said to Jesus, 'Rabbi, look! The fig tree you cursed has withered!'" Notice that Peter said to Jesus, "You cursed it." Just 24 hours later, the tree was totally dry and withered. The parallel passage in Matthew 21:20–21, recounting the same incident, says, "When the disciples saw this, they were amazed. 'How did the fig tree wither so quickly?' they asked. Jesus replied, 'I tell you the truth, if you have faith and do not doubt, not only can you do what was done to the fig tree, but also you can say to this mountain, "Go, throw yourself into the sea," and it will be done.'"

You see that Jesus authorized the disciples, too, to curse things. Acts 13:9–12 records that Paul did this when the sorcerer Elymas sought to keep Barnabas and him from speaking to the Roman proconsul. Yet this lesson seems to have been lost on most Christians. When we encounter such "fruitless fig trees," do we pass by unconcerned? Or do we take the same kind of aggressive action that Jesus demonstrated?

In Galatians 1:6–9 Paul curses those who bring heretical teachings to the Church. He says, "I am astonished that you are so quickly deserting the one who called you by the grace of Christ and are turning to a different gospel—which is really no gospel at all. . . . If anybody is preaching to you a gospel other than what you accepted, let him be eternally condemned!" A person who represents himself as a minister of Christ but perverts the central truth of the Gospel brings a curse *(anathema)* upon himself. In 2 Thessalonians 2:3 Paul warns that at the close of the age there will be widespread apostasy from the Christian faith.

It is well known that leaders in major Christian denominations have publicly renounced faith in the Scriptures and, in particular, in the bodily resurrection of Christ. Their declaration of unbelief is in itself a fulfillment of the Scriptures they are rejecting! Unless they repent, they bring upon themselves the wrath of God.

A curse must only be uttered by Christians when it is expressing the sovereign judgment of God. It must not proceed from the mind or will of the speaker, nor express human anger or vindictiveness. In Luke 9:51–56 we read that people in a Samaritan village refused to receive the disciples. In response, James and John asked Jesus, "Lord, do you want us to call fire down from heaven to destroy them?" (verse 54). However, Jesus rebuked them. Some manuscripts say that He added, "You do not know what kind of spirit you are of, for the Son of Man did not come to destroy people's lives, but to save them."

Note that Jesus knew that Elijah had called down fire to destroy his enemies, and He did not question whether James and John might have been able to do the same. Yet He rebuked them, emphasizing that under the New Covenant, God has chosen to use His servants primarily as instruments of mercy and not of judgment.

Study questions:

1. Give an example of an Old Testament curse fulfilled many years later.
2. How did Jesus authorize the disciples to curse things? What did the fig tree represent?
3. Give an example of a curse in the book of Acts.
4. When are curses by Christians justified?
5. Do you know of any examples of such a curse in your experience?

8

Self-Imposed Curses

Everyone who is concerned about their personal well-being should be aware of the frightening power of their own words. They can be like boomerangs that come flying back to strike the one who released them.

In Matthew 12:36–37 Jesus gives a solemn warning about the danger of words carelessly spoken. "I tell you that people will have to give account on the day of judgment for every careless word they have spoken. For by your words you will be acquitted, and by your words you will be condemned."

Jesus here focuses on careless words—those spoken idly, without premeditation. Even if we do not really mean them, they can have power. We need to remember that God takes our words seriously, even when we ourselves do not. One woman who was healed in her thirties of very irregular periods said that in her teenage years she and her peers had carelessly called menstruation "the curse."

Mark 14:66–72 records how, in the court of the high priest, Peter three times denied that he was a disciple of Jesus. To enforce his third denial, he actually "began to call down curses on himself, and he swore to them, 'I don't know this man you're talking about'" (verse 71). Although Peter was quickly stricken with remorse, it is doubtful that even then he understood the full implication of his own words. Three days later, at the empty tomb, the angels told the women, "Go, tell his disciples and Peter, 'He is going ahead of you into Galilee'" (Mark 16:7). Peter was no longer reckoned as one of the disciples. By his own words he had forfeited his standing as a disciple of Jesus.

Later, John 21:15–17 records how Jesus graciously reinstated Peter as His disciple. He asked Peter three times, "Do you love me?" Peter answered three times in the affirmative, but he was grieved that Jesus asked the question three times. He did not realize that Jesus was leading him in this way to revoke his previous denials. For each time that he had made a wrong confession, he now made the right confession.

This establishes a pattern for all who need to be released from the snare of a bad confession. We must repent, revoke and replace. First, we must acknowledge that we have spoken wrong words and repent of them. Second, we must unsay, or cancel, what was wrong. Third, we must replace our previous wrong confession the right one. These three steps, taken in faith, can release us the snare.

actually very common for people to pronounce curses upon lves. Remember the story in Genesis of Rebekah persuading obtain Isaac's blessing by deception? When Jacob was being found out, he said, "What if my father touches me? ppear to be tricking him and would bring down a curse rather than a blessing." His mother said to him, "My s , let the curse fall on me" (Genesis 27:12–13). Rebekah invited a curse to come upon herself, which kept her from enjoying the fruits of her success. Later on in a mood of pessimism, she complained to her husband, Isaac, that Esau had married wives she did not approve of. She said, "I'm disgusted with living because of these Hittite women. If Jacob takes a wife from among the women of this land, ... my life will not be worth living" (Genesis 27:46). Rebekah pronounced a double curse upon herself, effectively saying that she might as well die.

I cannot tell you how many people we have met who have cursed themselves this way. "What's life got to offer me? I might as well be dead." You do not have to say that very often. It is like an invitation to the spirit of death, and he does not need many invitations—he will come in. The devil is the one who tricks you into saying that—often for very inadequate reasons, such as a fit of pique or discouragement. Yet you are setting your own destiny!

We have seen scores of people delivered from the spirit of death that came in through such negative talk. At one meeting in Northern Ireland, I was speaking to an audience of about two thousand people, and I felt led to pray a collective prayer for people who needed deliverance from the spirit of death. About fifty people received deliverance simultaneously! Most of them were young people.

A much more tragic and far-reaching example of a self-imposed curse is described in Matthew 27:24–25. The scene is the trial of Jesus by Pontius Pilate. "When Pilate saw that he was getting nowhere, but that instead an uproar was starting, he took water and washed his hands in front of the crowd. 'I am innocent of this man's blood,' he said. 'It is your responsibility!' All the people answered, 'Let his blood be on us and on our children!' " That was a self-imposed curse of monumental proportions. You really cannot understand the history of the Jewish people over the last twenty centuries until you understand that one major factor is a self-imposed, perpetuating curse. "Let his blood be on us and on our children." In that context, the word "children" means each succeeding generation. How tragic!

Since 1989 I have been present at two meetings in Israel when Jewish leaders of Messianic congregations publicly confessed this sin on behalf of their people and asked God for release from it. Thank God, release is possible because on the cross Jesus prayed, "Father, forgive them, for they do not know what they are doing" (Luke 23:34).

The history of Israel provides a vivid example of words determining our destinies. In chapters 13 and 14 of Numbers, Moses sent twelve tribal leaders to spy out the land of Canaan, which God had promised to Israel as an inheritance. Two of them—Joshua and Caleb—returned with a positive report: "We should go up and take possession of the land, for we can certainly do it" (Numbers 13:30). The other ten spread a bad report that concluded, "We can't attack these people; they are stronger than we are" (verse 31).

The Lord told Moses and Aaron to tell the Israelites, "I will do to you the very things I heard you say" (Numbers 14:28). Those who said, "We are able to enter the land" did so. Those who said it was impossible did not. In the same way, God tells Christians, "I will do the very things I hear you say."

These are just some of the statements that may open you up to a curse: "You're driving me crazy!" "If there's a bug around, I'll catch it." "I just know my husband will be unfaithful." "I can never make ends meet." "Good things never happen to me." "I'm just clumsy." "Over my dead body!"

Pledges or oaths required for admission to a closed society are another way of invoking a curse against oneself. Once when my first wife, Lydia, and I were struggling to set a young woman free from demonic bondage, Lydia was prompted to tell the woman to take off her ring. As soon as she did so, she was immediately delivered. Lydia had not known that the ring was a college sorority ring. To join the sorority, the young woman had been required to make certain pledges inconsistent with her Christian faith. She needed to discard the ring to cancel those pledges and regain her liberty.

In Exodus 23:32–33 God warned Israel about the idolatrous nations whose land they were about to enter: "Do not make a covenant with them or with their gods. . . . The worship of their gods will certainly be a snare to you." If you make a very solemn agreement with people who are under the power of evil forces, you come under that same power. This is particularly true of secret societies such as the Ku Klux Klan in America, and the Freemasons worldwide. The latter is a sure road to disaster for your descendants. To be initiated, a person has to bind himself, by the most frightening and barbarous oaths, never to reveal any of freemasonry's secrets.

I once prayed for a woman in Australia whose father was a Freemason. Her baby was emaciated and ill, and she herself was unwell and unkempt. After she renounced the spirit of freemasonry, both mother and daughter underwent a dramatic change.

As Christians, we are all in a covenant relationship with the Lord, and the only other valid covenant is that of marriage between a husband and wife. Covenants are very powerful, and to enter into a covenant relationship on any other basis but these can be extremely dangerous. If it is a scriptural covenant, its effect will be a blessing. But if it is unscriptural, its effect will be a curse.

Solomon offers an urgent word of counsel in Proverbs 6:4–5 to anyone who has made a pledge or vow binding them to an evil association:

> Allow no sleep to your eyes,
> no slumber to your eyelids.
> Free yourself, like a gazelle from the hand of the hunter,
> like a bird from the snare of the fowler.

What you have said with your own lips only you can unsay. At the same time, get rid of any articles associated with the ungodly covenant. It is best to do this in the presence of Christian witnesses who can support you with their faith.

Study questions:

1. What did Jesus warn us about the words we use?
2. How did Peter curse himself with his own words? What was significant about the way Jesus reinstated him?

3. If we have cursed ourselves with our own words, which three steps should we take?
4. What kinds of statements might open you to a curse? Do you commonly make any of these?
5. What kinds of covenants are forbidden? What are the only two types of covenants appropriate for Christians?

9

Curses from Servants of Satan

In this section we will uncover another source of curses: servants of Satan.

Satan is a created being, a rebellious angel, who was cast out of God's heaven. He rules over a spiritual kingdom of evil angels, together with lesser evil spirits, who are collectively called demons. His name means "adversary" or "one who opposes." He is the implacable enemy of God Himself and the people and purposes of God. His aim is to control the entire human race, and his primary tactic is deception.

Although everyone in rebellion against God is being driven by Satan, there are some who have deliberately opened themselves up to satanic forces. Such people are recognized in most cultures and are known as witch doctors, medicine men, mchawi, shamans, tohanga, witches or priests or priestesses of Satan. Witch doctors are experts at curses—it is their profession.

Parts of Africa are totally dominated by witch doctors. Everything in people's lives is controlled by their unseen spiritual power. Once when our team was in Zambia, we offered to pray for barren women who could not have children. Out of a large group of about seven thousand people, about four hundred women in that condition came forward for prayer. Before we prayed for them we told the interpreter to ask them how many had been to a witch doctor to get a potion or a charm to enable them to have children. Out of the four hundred, there were only two who did not raise their hands.

When we came with this message about the release from the curse, it produced one of the most dramatic changes I have ever seen in people. After they had listened to my teaching and repeated the prayer of release after me, those people were visibly transformed. Up to that time you hardly saw them smile, but from then on they were some of the happiest people. The change was as from night to day.

Balaam is a biblical example of a witch doctor. The king of Moab knew he could not defeat Israel in war, so he hired Balaam to pronounce a curse on them. "For I know that those you bless are blessed, and those you curse are cursed" (Numbers 22:6). That is typical. Most African tribes preparing for battle will get the witch doctor to put a curse on their enemies. They then believe they will be able to defeat them.

Many Christians today would dismiss this as superstitious nonsense devoid of any real power. But God viewed the curses that Balaam might pronounce as a serious threat to Israel. Consequently, He intervened supernaturally. Even now God does not ignore or belittle curses directed against His people by servants of Satan. Jesus showed us that God recognizes the power of Satan but equips His servants with superior power.

In the mid-1980s a leader of the Satanic church in the United States was interviewed on television. When asked if Satanists practice human sacrifice, he replied that they destroyed human beings who would oppose them by proxy in the form of hexes and curses. There is also evidence of gruesome human sacrifice, including infants and small children, performed by satanic groups.

Primary targets of satanic curses and other occult weapons are the servants of God and Jesus Christ. Satanists recognize who their main enemies are and direct their attacks accordingly. We have become so civilized in some places that we do not believe these things are real. But they still have serious power to harm us.

"New Age" and occult activities

Many people voluntarily but unknowingly open themselves to curses by engaging in activities that have links with other religions or New Age practices. Because their true nature is concealed by deceptive terminology, they are appropriately described as occult (derived from a Latin word meaning "hidden" or "covered over"). These occult practices have always held a powerful fascination for fallen human beings, never more so than in the present generation. (Significantly, the word *fascination* comes from a Latin verb meaning "to bewitch.")

This is a highly complex area, but there are three main branches: witchcraft, divination and sorcery.

Witchcraft is the power branch of the occult, rooted in rebellion against God. It is a person's attempt to gain his own aims without submitting to God's law. Its driving force is a desire to control people and circumstances, either by psychological pressure or psychic techniques. Wherever people use verbal or nonverbal tactics to manipulate, intimidate and dominate those around them, witchcraft is at work.

In its simplest form, witchcraft is merely an expression of fallen humanity. In Galatians 5:20 it is listed—with idolatry—among "the acts of the sinful nature." There are probably few people who have not resorted at some time or another to attempts at manipulation and control. Yet it is characteristic of Satan that he exploits this as an opening for supernatural, demonic power that emanates from the kingdom of darkness. Through it he takes control of people and makes them tools of his evil purposes. The result is the occult art of witchcraft, operating through spells and curses.

In contemporary culture we may be exposed to witchcraft in the forms of acupressure, acupuncture, astral projection, hypnosis, levitation, martial arts that invoke supernatural spiritual power, mind control and telekinesis.

Divination is the knowledge branch of the occult, including all kinds of revelation that claim a non-Christian spiritual source. Its commonest form is fortune-telling, offering supernatural knowledge of the future. It also includes astrology, automatic writing, cabala, "channeling," clairaudience (hearing voices), clairvoyance, crystal ball gazing, diagnosis by color therapy or a pendulum, divining, ESP, handwriting analysis, horoscopes, iridology, mediums, mind reading, numerology, omens, palmistry, phrenology, séances, tarot cards, tea leaf reading, telepathy and "witching," as well as all books that teach occult practices.

Also included under this heading are all false religions or cults that claim supernatural revelation but contradict the Bible. Distinguishing between true and false in this realm is like distinguishing between straight and crooked in the natural realm. Once we have established a standard of what is straight, we know that anything departing from that standard is crooked. Whether it varies by one degree or ninety degrees, it is crooked. Some of the subtlest deceptions are those that appear to differ only a little from the Bible.

Particularly dangerous are religions that misrepresent the person, the nature or the redemptive work of Jesus Christ. Jehovah's Witnesses, for example, teach that Jesus was merely a created being, while Islam denies that Jesus was the Son of God or that He actually died on the cross. Modern cults include anthroposophy, Black Mass, "Children of God," Christadelphians, Christian Science, freemasonry, Mormonism (Church of the Latter Day Saints), Religious Science, Rosicrucianism, Scientology, Spiritual Frontiers Fellowship, Spiritualism, Theosophy, the Unification Church (Moonies, One World Crusade), the Unitarian Church and the Worldwide Church of God (founded by Herbert W. Armstrong).

Eastern religions such as Bahai, Buddhism, Confucianism, the Divine Light Mission, Hare Krishna, Hinduism, Shintoism, Transcendental Meditation and yoga also fall into this category as well as other aspects of the New Age movement.

Sorcery operates through material objects or other ways of influencing the physical senses, such as hallucinogenic drugs or music. In Revelation 9:21 the word for "magic arts" is derived directly from the Greek word for drugs. In 2 Timothy 3:13 Paul warns that at the close of the age "evil men and imposters will go from bad to worse, deceiving and being deceived." The word translated "impostors" means literally "enchanters." Chanting, or incantation, has always been a technique of sorcery. The contemporary drug and music culture is a vivid example of two forms of sorcery working together.

Amulets, ankhs (crosses with rings at the top), birthstones, charms (e.g., for wart removal), crystals used for healing, hex signs, "lucky" symbols such as inverted horseshoes, ouija boards, pagan fetishes or religious artifacts, planchettes, talismans, zodiac charms and even books can be channels of occult power. In Acts 19:18–19 we read that the Ephesians who had practiced sorcery burnt their scrolls, even though the value of the material destroyed was very great. The only appropriate way to deal with such occult material is to destroy it completely.

Study questions:

1. What is Satan's purpose in relation to God?
2. Which people have intentionally opened themselves up to satanic curses? Give a biblical example of a witch doctor.
3. Are there people in Western societies who use satanic curses and other occult weapons? Who are their primary targets?
4. What did Jesus teach about God's attitude toward curses from servants of Satan?
5. Have you inadvertently exposed yourself to occult influences?

10

Soulish Prayers or Utterances

Many Christians would be surprised to learn that they can be harmed by spiritual forces emanating from their fellow believers. James says, "But if you harbor bitter envy and selfish ambition in your hearts, do not boast about it or deny the truth. Such 'wisdom' does not come down from heaven but is earthly, unspiritual, of the devil" (James 3:14–15). Ungodly wisdom has three characteristics—it is earthly, it is unspiritual and, finally, it is demonic. The Greek word here translated "unspiritual" is from the root *psyche*, meaning soul. The word *soulish* is used elsewhere in the New Testament to describe the activity of the human soul when it is out of right relationship to the spirit.

In Jude 16–19 the apostle describes a class of persons who are associated with the Church but are nevertheless "grumblers and faultfinders; they follow their own evil desires" (verse 16). He concludes by saying of them, "These are the people who divide you, who follow mere natural instincts and do not have the Spirit" (verse 19). The New Testament gives very clear warnings to Christians as to how they should speak about other people, and especially their fellow believers. In Titus 3:2 Paul says that we are to "slander no one." One Greek verb translated "to slander," or "to speak evil" is *blasphemo*—from which is derived the word *blaspheme*. The sin of blasphemy includes not only evil words spoken against God, but also evil words spoken against our fellow human beings.

James deals specifically with words that Christians speak about one another: "Brothers, do not slander one another" (James 4:11). The word here translated "slander" is *katalalo*, which means simply "to speak against." Many Christians interpret this to mean we are not to say anything false against other believers. What he actually says, however, is that we are not to speak against fellow believers at all—even if what we say about them is true.

This includes gossip, which is classed by many Christians as a relatively harmless practice. Yet in Romans 1:29–30, Paul groups it with many serious sins. Christians criticizing one another and running one another down generate a negative power against the people they talk about. The words would not normally be described as "curses," but their effect is the same. Furthermore, the believer who is guilty of this kind of speech defiles himself as well as that part of the Body of Christ to which he is related.

There are some prayers you would be better off without. That sounds shocking, but some people seek to control you by their prayers. They have their own ideas about where you should live, whom you should marry or what form your ministry should take. Yet their ideas do not come from God. They generate a soulish pressure that may even be demonic and that keeps you from finding what God's will really is for you.

Proverbs 28:9 warns us, "If anyone turns a deaf ear to the law, even his prayers are detestable." It is possible for prayers to be motivated by envy and self-seeking, resentment, anger, criticism or self-righteousness. When prayers accuse or are used to dominate or manipulate others, they are particularly dangerous. They will not be received by the Father and instead can have an earthly, even demonic, force attached to them.

If we have been guilty of speaking against one another or praying wrongly, we need to repent and seek God's forgiveness. We may also need to ask forgiveness from people who have been affected by the negative influence of our speech and prayers and renounce any such behavior for the future.

Study questions:

1. What does the word *soulish,* or "unspiritual," mean when it is used in the New Testament?
2. What do Paul and James say about gossip or slander?
3. In what way can the sin of blasphemy be more widely defined?
4. How can someone's prayers have a negative effect?
5. Have you been guilty of speaking against someone or praying wrongly? What should you do about it?

11

The Divine Exchange

Through the death of Jesus on the cross, God has made full provision for every human need, including release from a curse. "Christ redeemed us from the curse of the law by becoming a curse for us, for it is written: 'Cursed is everyone who is hung on a tree.' He redeemed us in order that the blessing given to Abraham might come to the Gentiles through Christ Jesus, so that by faith we might receive the promises of the Spirit" (Galatians 3:13–14). The atonement was a divine exchange: All the evil due to us came upon Christ so that all the good due to Him might be made available to us. He was wounded that we might be healed. He died that we might have life. He was made sin that we might be made righteous. He was rejected that we might be accepted. In particular, He was made a curse that we might enter into the blessing.

In verse 13 the word *curse* appears three times. "Christ redeemed us from the curse of the law by becoming a curse for us, for it is written: 'Cursed is everyone who is hung on a tree.'" If Christ had to be made a curse on the cross for us, then do not entertain the thought that there is no reality in a curse. God would not have made provision at such cost if there was nothing to be delivered from. It took the substitutionary sacrifice of Jesus Christ to provide deliverance from the curse.

There is no other basis of our deliverance but faith in what Christ has done for us on the cross. Just as we are made righteous because He was made sin, so we can receive the blessing because He was made the curse. The Law of Moses says in Deuteronomy 21:23 that anyone hung on a tree becomes a curse. Every Jew who knew the Law of Moses would have realized that Jesus was made a curse when they saw Him hanging on a cross.

The purpose accomplished by Jesus' sacrifice is summed up in Isaiah 53:6:

We all, like sheep, have gone astray,
    each of us has turned to our own way;
and the Lord has laid on him
    the iniquity of us all.

The Hebrew word here translated "iniquity" is *avon*, which describes not only sin but also the punishment or evil consequences that sin brings in its wake. Like an animal offering brought to the temple as a guilt offering to carry the people's sin, Jesus took away the sin of the whole world, and with it the punishment—the curse.

► *His righteousness for our sin*
In 2 Corinthians 5:21 Paul presents the positive side of the exchange: "God made him who had no sin to be sin for us, so that in him we might become the righteousness of God." This righteousness is not something that we can achieve by our own efforts, but a divine righteousness that has never known sin. None of us can ever earn this. It is as high above our own righteousness as heaven is above earth. It can be received solely by faith.

► *His life for our death*
In Hebrews 2:9 the writer says that Jesus tasted death for everyone. Jesus died our death that we might share His life. In James 1:15 the apostle says, "Sin, when it is full-grown, gives birth to death." Death is part of the curse that Jesus removed through His death on the cross so that we could experience life in all its fullness.

► *His healing for our wounds*
As Jesus hung on the cross, Isaiah 53:4–5 says, He "took up our infirmities and carried our sorrows," and "by his wounds we are healed." Just as He took our spiritual sickness, He also took our physical sicknesses upon His body so that through His pain we might be healed. Matthew 8:16–17 refers back to this passage and says that Jesus "drove out the spirits with a word and healed all the sick. This was to fulfill what was spoken through the prophet Isaiah." Physical healing, then, is part of the work of Jesus that we receive through His death.

► *His riches for our poverty*
Another aspect of the divine exchange is stated in 2 Corinthians 8:9: "For you know the grace of our Lord Jesus Christ, that though he was rich, yet for your sakes he became poor, so that you through his poverty might become rich." Although Jesus is often

thought of as being poor throughout His earthly ministry, in fact He exemplified abundance. He had all He needed to do the will of God in His life, continually giving out to others, and His supply was never exhausted. But it was on the cross that Jesus experienced absolute poverty. Hungry, thirsty, naked and in need of all things, He became utterly poor so that we could have abundance.

▶ *His glory and acceptance for our shame and rejection*
Finally, the divine exchange covers all the emotional forms of suffering that have followed the Fall. Two of the cruelest wounds brought upon us by sin are shame and rejection: Both came upon Jesus in His crucifixion. The writer of Hebrews says that He "endured the cross, scorning its shame" (Hebrews 12:2). Execution on a cross was the most shameful of all forms of death, reserved for the lowest class of criminal. The person to be executed was stripped of all his clothing and exposed naked to the gaze of jeering passers-by.

In taking on our sin, Jesus also suffered something even more excruciating—rejection and separation from His heavenly Father. Matthew 27:46 records, "About the ninth hour Jesus cried out in a loud voice, '*Eloi, Eloi, lama sabachthani?*'—which means, 'My God, my God, why have you forsaken me?'" So many people in our contemporary society are suffering from shame and rejection. These crippling wounds often stem from abuse or damaged relationships in childhood or later experiences such as the breakup of a marriage. Yet healing flows from the cross of Jesus. He bore our shame that we might share His glory. He endured our rejection so that we could have full acceptance as children of God.

There is no need resulting from human rebellion that is not covered by the same principle of divine exchange: Evil came upon Jesus so that good might come to us. He became a curse that we might receive the blessing.

The fullness of salvation

The divine exchange could be summed up in one grand, all-inclusive word: *salvation*. Christians often limit salvation to the experience of having one's sins forgiven and being born again. Yet this is only the first part of the total salvation revealed in the New Testament.

In the original Greek text, the verb *sozo*, normally translated "to save," is used in many ways that go beyond the forgiveness of sins.

It is often used in cases of people being physically healed (see Matthew 9:21–22; Mark 5:23; Luke 8:48; Acts 4:9; James 5:15 and other passages). It is also used of a person being delivered from demons (Luke 8:36) and of a dead person being brought back to life (Luke 8:50). In the case of Lazarus, it is used of recovering from a fatal illness (John 11:12). In 2 Timothy 4:18 Paul uses the same verb to describe God's ongoing preservation and protection from evil.

The total outworking of salvation includes every part of a person's being. It is beautifully summed up in Paul's prayer in 1 Thessalonians 5:23: "May God himself, the God of peace, sanctify you through and through. May your whole spirit, soul and body be kept blameless at the coming of our Lord Jesus Christ." Salvation includes the total human personality and is consummated only by the resurrection of the body at the return of Christ. No one enters into the varied provisions of salvation simultaneously or in one single transaction. It is normal to progress by stages, as the Holy Spirit guides. Very often a curse over a person's life is the unsuspected barrier that holds him back from the other provisions of salvation, and this barrier must be dealt with first.

Give thanks

If you are living under the shadow of a curse, have you begun to see that Jesus, at infinite cost to Himself, has made full provision for your release? If so, make a simple response of faith by saying, "Thank You!"

Right now, tell Him, "Thank You, Lord Jesus, for all You have done for me. I do not fully understand, but I do believe, and I am grateful." Keep thanking Him with your own words. The more you thank Him, the more you will believe what He has done for you. And the more you believe, the more you will want to thank Him.

Giving thanks is the first step to release.

Study questions:

1. How did Jesus become a curse for us?
2. How can you explain the "divine exchange"?
3. What are the blessings of salvation that flow from the cross?
4. Is there a shadow over your life that holds you back from receiving all that God wants to provide for you?
5. What is the first step to release from a curse?

12

How to Pass from Curse to Blessing

Through the death of Jesus, release from any curse is already legally ours—He has already obtained it for us. What we have to do is move from the legal to the experiential; we have to get it working in our lives. God does not have to do anything more, but we have to appropriate what God has already done for us. There are certain simple steps you need to follow.

Very often we need to ascertain the cause or the source of the curse—not always, but very often. As you have been reading this book, I am trusting that the Holy Spirit will speak to you. You may suddenly see, perhaps by supernatural revelation, the reason why you have struggled all your life under the shadow of a curse. In many cases, God wants us to know what we are being released from and how it came upon us. If God shows you, then act on it.

The basic pattern is stated in four simple words:

- *Recognize* your problem and its cause.
- *Repent* of anything that ever opened you to it.
- *Renounce* the curse.
- *Resist* every attempt of Satan to keep you under the curse.

Specific steps

1. Confess your faith in Christ and in His sacrifice on your behalf
In Romans 10:9–10 Paul explains that there are two essential conditions for receiving the benefits of Jesus' sacrifice: to believe in your heart that God raised Jesus from the dead and to confess (speak out) with your mouth that He is Lord. Faith is not fully effective until it has been completed by confession. This means that we are declaring what God has already said in His Word.

In Hebrews 3:1 Jesus is called the "high priest whom we confess." When we make the right scriptural confession, it releases His priestly ministry on our behalf.

58

This confession must be specific and personal. For example:

Lord Jesus Christ, I believe that You are the Son of God and the only way to God, and that You died on the cross for my sins and rose again from the dead.

2. Repent of all your rebellion and sins

There may have been many external factors, even going back to previous generations that have contributed to the curse over your life. Nevertheless, you must take personal responsibility for any sin that affects you. Before you can receive God's mercy, you must decide to repent—to lay down your rebellion and submit yourself unreservedly to all that God requires of you. A person who has truly repented does not argue with God!

Here is a suggested confession:

I give up all my rebellion and all my sin, and I submit myself to You as Lord. I turn to You, Lord Jesus, for mercy. From now on I want to live for You. I want to hear Your voice and do what You tell me.

3. Claim forgiveness of all sins

The great barrier that keeps God's blessing out of our lives is unforgiven sin. Confess any known sins of your own or your ancestors and ask God for His forgiveness. You are not personally guilty for any sins your ancestors have committed, but you are affected by their consequences. For example, you may need to confess, "My aunt was a fortune-teller," or "My grandfather was in Christian Science," or "My father is a Freemason." You have to identify yourself with the sin in your family that brought the curse upon your family. You confess that sin on behalf of your family and renounce it.

A suitable prayer would be:

I confess all my sins before You and ask for Your forgiveness. I especially ask forgiveness for any sins that exposed me to a curse, whether committed by me or by my ancestors or others related to me.

4. Forgive all other persons, including anyone who was the cause of the curse

If you do not forgive, unforgiveness is a barrier to the answer of your prayer. Jesus said, "And when you stand praying, if you hold anything against anyone, forgive him, so that your Father in heaven may forgive you your sins" (Mark 11:25). That leaves out nothing and nobody. Remember, forgiveness is a decision; it is not an emotion. Simply put, it is tearing up the IOUs.

Imagine that someone else owes you ten thousand dollars. You want it back, but meanwhile, you are reminded that you owe God ten million dollars. God offers to get rid of your debt, provided you forgive the other person his debt. If you persist in holding onto the other person's debt, though, God assures you that He will hold onto yours. Understood this way, forgiving another person is not a tremendous sacrifice—it is merely enlightened self-interest!

Ask the Holy Spirit to bring to mind anyone whom you need to forgive. Respond to His prompting and specifically name each person. Remember, the ones you find hardest to forgive are the ones you most need to forgive. You can use these words:

> By a decision of my will, I forgive all who have harmed me or wronged me, just as I want God to forgive me. In particular, I forgive [name those whom you need to forgive].

5. Renounce all contact with the occult or with secret societies

Remind yourself of the different occult and satanic activities listed earlier. If you have been involved in any of them, even against your will, you must renounce them. This includes any secret societies such as freemasonry or the Ku Klux Klan. Make a complete break from all such activities and practices.

In 2 Corinthians 6 Paul says, "What fellowship can light have with darkness? What harmony is there between Christ and Belial [Satan]? . . . What agreement is there between the temple of God and idols? . . . 'Therefore come out from them and be separate,' says the Lord. 'Touch no unclean thing and I will receive you'" (verses 14–15, 17). Making this break requires also that you deal with any "contact objects." You cannot keep in your house anything that binds you to the occult—including images, charms, statues of Buddha, tarot cards, etc. Moses warned the Israelites that if they took an accursed thing into their houses, they would become accursed like the thing (Deuteronomy 7:26). Get rid of it in the most effective way: burn it, smash it, throw it into deep water—or whatever!

[handwritten margin notes: "very IMPORTANT"; "very IMPORTANT"; "without? IMPORTANT"]

If you are ready to make this total break with Satan and his kingdom, here is an appropriate way to affirm it:

> I renounce all contact with anything occult or satanic or any secret society that binds me against the will of my Father God. I commit myself to remove from my house any objects linked to these forbidden areas or activities. I cancel all Satan's claims against me.

6. You are now ready to pray for release from any curse

Release yourself in the name of Jesus. The Word of God says that whatever we release on earth will be released in heaven and whatever we bind on earth shall be bound in heaven (see Matthew 18:18). You can say:

> *Lord Jesus, I believe that on the cross You took on Yourself every curse that could ever come upon me. So I now release myself from every curse, every evil influence and every dark shadow over me or my family, from any source whatsoever, in Your name, Jesus Christ.*
>
> *By faith I now receive my release and I thank You for it. Amen*

Study questions:

1. What does recognition of sin and confession have to do with release from a curse?
2. Why should we identify ourselves with the sin of others in praying for release?
3. Explain the importance of forgiveness and renunciation.
4. Do you need to take any practical steps to free yourself from curses?
5. Are you ready to pray the prayer of release?

The Prayer of Release

Now that you have read all of the preceding material, you would be wise to reaffirm each of the confessions you have already made before praying the prayer of release in its entirety. They are reprinted below to make it simpler for you.

Read them out loud, slowly and deliberately, in the presence of supportive witnesses if that would help you. If you feel uncertainty about any section, go back and read it again. Identify yourself with the words you utter. You should have the sense that you have brought yourself to God with the words you have spoken.

Lord Jesus Christ, I believe that You are the son of God and the only way to God, and that You died on the cross for my sins and rose again from the dead.

I give up all my rebellion and all my sin, and I submit myself to You as Lord. I turn to You, Lord Jesus, for mercy. From now on I want to live for You. I want to hear Your voice and do what You tell me.

I confess all my sins before You and ask for Your forgiveness. I especially ask forgiveness for any sins that exposed me to a curse, whether committed by me or by my ancestors or others related to me [add personal details that are appropriate].

By a decision of my will, I forgive all who have harmed me or wronged me, just as I want God to forgive me. In particular, I forgive [add any names that are appropriate].

I renounce all contact with anything occult or satanic or any secret society that binds me against the will of my Father God. I commit myself to remove from my house any objects linked to these forbidden areas or activities. I cancel all Satan's claims against me.

Lord Jesus, I believe that on the cross You took on Yourself every curse that could ever come upon me. So I now release myself from every curse, every evil influence and every dark shadow over me or my family, from any source whatsoever, in Your name, Jesus Christ.

By faith I now receive my release and I thank You for it. Amen!

Close by thanking God

After a prayer like that, the purest and simplest expression of faith is to begin thanking God from the bottom of your heart. Here are some ways you can thank God.

I thank You, Lord, that You have heard my prayer and that every curse over my life has been revoked and canceled.

I thank You, Lord, that I have been delivered from the domain of darkness and translated into the Kingdom of Your love.

I thank You that Satan has no more claims against me or my family or anything else that You have committed to me.

I thank You, Lord, that from now on, as I walk in obedience, Your blessings will come upon me and overtake me.

Now, believe that you have received. Open yourself to all the blessing God has for you. Keep reaffirming the scriptural truths and promises that you have already declared if you sense any kind of oppression in the future. Commit yourself to continue following the Lord and listening to His Spirit.

And now, as you set your face toward the land of God's blessings, receive the admonition given three times to Joshua: "Be strong and courageous. Do not be terrified; do not be discouraged, for the LORD your God will be with you wherever you go" (Joshua 1:9).

Derek Prince was born in India of British parents. He was educated as a scholar of Greek and Latin at Eton College and Cambridge University, England, where he held a Fellowship in Ancient and Modern Philosophy at King's College. He also studied Hebrew and Aramaic, both at Cambridge University and the Hebrew University in Jerusalem. In addition, he speaks a number of other modern languages.

While serving with the British army in World War II, he began to study the Bible and experienced a life-changing encounter with Jesus Christ. Out of this encounter he formed two conclusions: first, that Jesus Christ is alive; second, that the Bible is a true, relevant, up-to-date book. These conclusions altered the whole course of his life. Since then, he has devoted his life to studying and teaching the Bible.

His daily radio broadcast, *Keys to Successful Living*, reaches more than half the world and includes translations into Arabic, Chinese, Croatian, Malagasy, Mongolian, Russian, Samoan, Spanish and Tongan. He is the author of over 40 books, over 450 audio and 150 video teaching cassettes, many of which have been translated and published in more than 60 languages.

Derek's main gift is explaining the Bible and its teaching in a clear and simple way. His nondenominational, nonsectarian approach has made his teaching equally relevant and helpful to people from all racial and religious backgrounds.